The Cu[re to] Emotional Unavailability

Discover the source of emotional unavailability, heal and have positive, successful relationships.

Stella Smith

www.ThePositiveRelationship.com

ISBN: 1723040444
ISBN-13: 978-1723040443

DEDICATION

This book is dedicated to all those who are or who love someone who is emotionally unavailable. It is possible to understand why people become emotionally unavailable and change.

Due to the volume, it takes some time,
but I do answer every email I receive through my website.
Visit www.ThePositiveRelationship.com and click on the
"contact me" tab!

6 Workbooks with 48 lessons that will change your life.
www.ThePositiveRelationship.com

Visit my website at www.ThePositiveRelationship.com to get more information or to get my $97.00 course which includes 6 digital workbooks comprised of 48 step-by-step lessons and printable worksheets.

CONTENTS

ACKNOWLEDGMENTS

Thank you to all of those clients that have shared their stories with me and done the hard work of becoming emotionally available to their partners, families and friends.

It has been a true pleasure helping you to overcome emotional unavailability and be able to have positive relationships in your life. Because of you I know there is hope for everyone who feels disconnected or unable to have a successful relationship.

Introduction

Nineteen years. That's how long Abby was married to an emotionally unavailable man. She begged, pleaded, cajoled, offered to go to counseling with him, went to counseling without him, compensated, accepted, loved, educated, tried to have a sex-filled marriage but ended up with a sexless marriage. Sadly, the relationship ended in divorce.

Not content with having one long-term relationship with an emotionally unavailable partner, after a year of being single, Abby started dating someone who seemed to be different on the outside but underneath was just as emotionally unavailable as her husband had been.

She asked me if she was only attracted to emotionally unavailable men. Her relationship history would undoubtedly say yes. I helped her learn what is it that made her attracted to that type of partner. I helped her break the cycle.

The truth is that many people end up in a relationship with an emotionally available partner because they are emotionally unavailable as well. I knew that change was possible for an emotionally unavailable person and that they could become emotionally available and have positive, healthy relationships.

Change is possible by learning about and addressing why you became emotional unavailable. Since it is a state of being, you can commit to being emotionally available and being with someone who is willing to be emotionally available in return.

As a certified Life Coach, I help people face their inner conflicts, heal and go on to have successful, fulfilling relationships. People can and do face their pain, shame and find ways to trust again in the context of healthy relationships.

Whether you are emotionally unavailable or someone you love is, it is possible to discover the reason for the unavailability and overcome it!

No one is destined from birth to experience failed relationship after failed relationship. We all have the ability, with some help, to figure out what is causing the pain and to get healing in that area. It does not have to be a permanent relationship death sentence.

People who struggle with emotional unavailability are emotionally hibernating, and it is possible to wake up from that deep emotional sleep.

When Sleeping Beauty was kissed by Prince Charming, she opened her eyes to her happily forever after. I'm not suggesting that becoming emotionally unavailable is instantaneous.

However, after helping hundreds of people overcome the emotionally unavailable state of being and move into a more healthy state of being, I can unequivocally affirm that those who want change *can change.*

This book is broken into two sections. The first section outlines the signs and behaviors of the emotionally unavailable person. It explains how a person becomes emotionally unavailable.

The second section of the book describes the different ways a person can heal from emotional unavailability and includes ideas to work on each of those areas.

On my website, www.ThePositiveRelationship.com you'll find more exercises and a workbook you can use if you want step-by-step guidance to self-help your way into emotional availability.

This book is written for both the emotionally unavailable who want to heal and to those who care about someone who is struggling in this area. It is my greatest desire that you find help and hope in overcoming emotional unavailability. There are tools for you to self-heal. Why not you, why not now?

Due to the volume, it may take a while, but I do answer every email sent to me through my website, www.ThePositiveRelationship.com. Just click the contact me link at the top of the page.

With much love and belief in your power to overcome emotional unavailability,

Stella Smith

Certified Master Life Coach

Certified Rational Emotive Behavioral Life Coach

Certified Cognitive Behavioral Life Coach

Certified Relationship Workshop Facilitator

Certified Life Purpose Life Coach

Certified Goal to Success Life Coach

Certified Public Speaking Training & Facilitator

Certified NLP Master Practitioner

Visit my website at www.ThePositiveRelationship.com to get more information.

PART ONE
The Problem of Emotional Unavailability.

Chapter One:
What Is Emotional Unavailability?

Men don't cry. Isn't that what most of us think when it comes to emotional unavailability? The fact is an emotionally unavailable person, male or female, can sob their way through a movie, even a Disney movie, with the best of us. They may be able to cry through films and TV shows all the time but for events in their life that ought to have impacted them emotionally, they may be unable to express emotion.

Being emotionally available to a partner and being able to express emotion are two different things.

Being emotionally available is not about being dramatic. It's not about being over-emotional. In fact, being dramatic or overly emotional is a coping mechanism meant to control the other person or situation.

A great example of this is on the sports court. A player misses a ball. They begin to beat on themselves emotionally in a pronounced way. It's tough for a coach to address the issue of why they missed the ball so that they can improve when a player is upset and berating themselves already.

But, the athlete in this example isn't truly upset with him or herself; they don't want the coach or other players talk to them about their actions. They miss out on a coachable moment that could help them improve by putting up an emotional wall that prevents real communication about what did happen and how to fix it. They control the situation, so they don't have to change, listen, feel rejected, feel embarrassed, or take responsibility.

Emotional unavailability is a distancing mechanism. It is a way to hide, so you never risk rejection. It is a way of rejecting the other person before they reject you.

An emotionally unavailable person can say "I love you," but they are really not capable of loving you because a deep level of emotional connection is just too frightening.

The emotionally unavailable person is capable of having a relationship, even a long-term one. Many can and do. Experts estimate that a significant portion of the population is emotionally unavailable. Many, many of those people are in relationships.

Emotionally unavailable people are capable of being in a relationship but not capable of being *present* in the relationship. They are not capable of truly loving the person they are with because, ultimately, they are unable or unwilling to love themselves or to risk being hurt. Some report they feel "emotionally dead" inside.

How does a person become emotionally unavailable?

1. You were born.

2. Along the way to becoming an adult, you experienced pain, rejection, and fear.

3. You developed coping strategies to manage the pain, rejection, and fear.

4. The coping strategies protected you from emotional pain, and that felt good.

5. But like the plant from the movie *The Little Shop of Horrors*, these coping strategies wanted to grow and screamed: "FEED ME!"

6. When you experienced fear, pain or conflict you relied on the comfort of the coping mechanisms rather than on being uncomfortable and facing the pain, fear or rejection.

7. The coping mechanisms now prevented authentic relationship because they are easy and facing your fear, anxiety and trusting other people is HARD.

8. The person you're with never gets the commitment of being with the real you, just a version of you cloaked in defense mechanisms because it is more comfortable. Ultimately you believe that they will reject or hurt you and eventually confirm what you think about yourself is true.

9. The person that loves you can see this is happening. They fight against it, but they will never win because how you feel is your responsibility, not theirs. And at some point, they decide that if you loved them you would be willing to address this in your life and even if they don't leave the relationship, they may give up on you.

10. This self-fulfilling prophecy confirms what you've believed all along. That risking loving another human being and having a genuine, authentic, emotionally open relationship leads to pain and rejection. You make your partner the problem and cement a lifelong commitment to emotional unavailability and ultimately being alone whether you are in a relationship or not.

When you are emotionally available, you don't use coping strategies to hide your real self or your feelings.

- It means connecting with the people you love in an authentic way.

- It is being open with yourself and your partner.

- It is telling the truth about how you really feel.

- It is giving up control of how someone might view or react to you.

- It is being able to commit to the relationship genuinely.

- It is addressing your secret shame and not letting your inner critic control you or the relationship.

- It is taking responsibility for your feelings and not viewing the other person as the problem.

There are hundreds of blogs out there that list "Top ten signs you're dating an emotionally unavailable person." Some of the signs are correct, and some are completely wrong. The often named "sign" I disagree with the most? Tardiness.

I know quite a few emotionally available people that are always running behind and, conversely, quite a few emotionally unavailable people that are right on time or even early to everything.

Habitual tardiness is a sign of procrastination, a life that is too busy to squeeze everything in, over commitment, a sign of chronic stress, or possibly even laziness.

As the typical emotionally unavailable person wants to avoid conflict, being late on purpose, which would lead to conflict, does not seem like a likely sign of emotional unavailability. Emotionally unavailable people can be chronically late like many other people in the general population; it's a personal bad habit or indication of a busy, unbalanced life. That's it.

As a Life Coach who has helped hundreds of people become emotionally available, another issue I have with the excessive number of "Top ten signs you're with an emotionally unavailable person" blog posts is that they all seem geared toward someone who is just starting a dating relationship and are typically written from the female perspective only.

Contrary to popular belief, emotional unavailability does not magically go away when you get married. In fact, I would argue now that the chase is over the emotionally unavailable person becomes even more emotionally unavailable. They no longer must be on their "best behavior," so any façade of being emotionally available slips away.

I point to the high rate of divorce as evidence that emotionally unavailable people *can and do* get married.

Experts will tell us that the reasons people fight and eventually divorce are money, sex and children. Emotionally unavailable people will seek to avoid pain and responsibility in all these areas.

Not only ought the signs of emotional unavailability to include symptoms within the context of a long-term relationship, but they ought to be written from a more gender neutral point of view. Because while it is true that many men are emotionally unavailable, women are as well.

Both men and women can be narcissists or can be capable of emotional abuse. For most blog posts listing signs of emotional unavailability to be pointed exclusively at men is unfortunate and inaccurate.

When we believe that emotional unavailability is a male-only problem (like prostate cancer) we do a disservice to millions of women who could gain awareness, move toward emotional health, and save their relationships with the people they love. Believing the idea that only men can be emotionally unavailable also shortchanges the men who love and need their partners to connect.

Since emotional unavailability is a problem of overly self-protecting because of the way you feel about yourself, let's define it as it really is: It's the way a person, male or female, hides from being vulnerable.

Chapter Two:
The Different Types of Emotionally Unavailable People.

When it comes to emotional unavailability, one size does not fit all.

There are:

- Emotionally unavailable people who behave passively in a relationship.

- Emotionally unavailable people who behave aggressively in a relationship.

- Emotionally unavailable people who will never commit to the other person in the relationship.

- Emotionally unavailable people who will commit to the other person in the relationship.

Most information on the internet describes an aggressive, emotionally unavailable male in the dating phase of the relationship. It's certainly true that an emotionally unavailable person can come on strong and then become cold. It's equally valid that a passive, emotionally unavailable person can lead you on for quite a long time before you realize that he or she will never formalize the relationship.

Personality and gifting, as well as upbringing, life circumstances and situational stress, all play their part in determining how an emotionally unavailable person will react in the context of a relationship.

As a relationship progresses, the way an emotionally unavailable person relates can change. Since their coping mechanisms are in overprotection mode, those coping mechanisms can change as the situation develops, or as the emotionally available partner attempts to connect.

Given that some emotionally unavailable people will never be able to commit beyond the dating phase, while others will be able to commit to marriage but be mostly absent in the relationship, I have outlined both "signs you're dating" and "signs you are in a long-term relationship" with an emotionally unavailable person. Both passive and aggressive personality tendencies for both relational situations are addressed.

An aggressive emotionally unavailable person might come on strong, declaring, "I love you" before they even know you. They want to proceed to sex without an intimate connection to support it.

A passive emotionally unavailable person might keep the pace of the relationship so slow you'll feel like you are in the "get to know you" phase for the entire life of the relationship.

As you read through the signs listed, some will apply, some may not. Whether passive or aggressive, dating or long-term, foundationally all emotional unavailability is anchored in self-protection.

As one savvy client put it, "It's an excuse for not committing to the relationship and trusting the other person not to hurt them."

Chapter Three:
The Non-Committers: Signs You May Be Dating an Emotionally Unavailable Person.

Passive and aggressive signs you are dating an emotionally unavailable person. Personality type determines which behaviors may be employed.

1. **They control contact frequency.** In the initial weeks of starting any new dating relationship, it's common for people only to connect every few days. But after the first few initial weeks pass most healthy relationships move toward touching base daily.

    Whether that's a friendly, "good morning" text or check-in call at night, normal relationships move toward communication and connection. At the beginning of a relationship, many people don't want to overwhelm the other party or make it seem like they're stalking them or are desperate.

    When emotionally healthy relationships are moving toward learning about each other and integrating the relationship into their lives, the emotionally unavailable person is still looking for space.

Everyone gets busy at work, gets sick, or has other life interruptions, but the emotionally unavailable person needs that to create space and emotional distance.

Sometimes limiting communication can be a way of slowing a relationship down to a reasonable pace, but sometimes it means the other person doesn't have room for you in their life. After the initial dating phase in an emotionally healthy dating relationship, it's normal to touch base in some way every day.

2. **You do not receive an invitation to social events.** After the first few weeks of any dating relationship, it is reasonable for you to become your partner's automatic "plus one." If you're surprised to find out they attended a wedding, a Fourth of July barbecue, or social event without you, it's possible you might need to think about why.

It could be just a simple as they RSVP'ed to the wedding before they met you and there is no way to change the guest count. If the relationship is new, they may not be ready to introduce you to their family especially if kids are involved.

They may have regular sports tickets that don't include the option of getting an extra seat. It would be ridiculous and awkward if a man were to be invited to a girl's night out just because they started dating a woman who was going to attend one.

There are plausible reasons why people don't invite their new significant other to attend an event with them. An emotionally healthy person lets the other person know about the upcoming event and why an invitation will not be extended to them.

In a dating relationship with an emotionally unavailable partner, you might find that three months after you started dating they still do not invite you to their social events. They are not ready and may never be prepared to acknowledge you to their friends or family.

After several months of seeing each other, you might be casually chatting when you are surprised to find out that they attended a wedding the previous weekend without you. You start to feel like you are excluded or hidden. If the only time you spend with your dating partner is solo, then there is a good chance that they are married or are emotionally unavailable.

3. **You haven't met the family.** If you've been dating more than three months and you haven't met your partner's family that is a huge red flag. Sometimes people don't introduce their partners to their family, not because they

want to hide them, but because they're protecting you from their family.

They may think if you knew what a dysfunctional group their family was, you wouldn't date them anymore. Some people have broken contact with their family, and so they have no one to introduce you to.

If your partner's family lives a considerable distance away, this can also contribute to a lack of introduction. But in an emotionally healthy relationship you meet your partner's family. It is a tricky situation because often you may excuse this lack of introduction as a sign that they are just not ready.

Someone who is committed to you will be ready sooner rather than later. If six months into the relationship you haven't met your dating partner's family, even over the phone, in the case of long-distance relationships, you probably never will.

4. **They won't leave any of their things at your place.**
Having stuff at your home would feel too much like a relationship instead of casual dating. Not only will they not offer you any space at their house for a few overnight things, but they also make you feel like it's a huge thing to ask. And if they concede to giving you a drawer, you feel

they do it grudgingly or give you a drawer that's well hidden.

5. **They won't go away with you.** A weekend away can give you time to get to know the other person on a deeper level and build closeness. The emotionally unavailable person wants to slow things down as much as possible, and building closeness is not their goal. Besides, weekends are to spend socializing with other people and not you.

6. **You only see them when you go away.** The opposite of never going away with the person you're dating is always going away. People that don't want to include you in their everyday life but still want sex might only see you when you're going out of town.

   It's fun to try a restaurant in another city or to go away for the weekend and share new experiences. But if every date involves going to a place where you won't run into anyone you know it's possible that the person you are dating is hiding you. And this is a relationship that won't be going anywhere.

7. **They talk about money in a harsh or judgmental way.** They'll spend money on themselves and be generous with others but will make comments when you're with them about not wanting to spend too much money. They seem to have a hypersensitivity about being used for their

money and adopt a harsh tone when mentioning it. They tell you outright, or you get the impression they feel bitter about being financially hurt.

There's almost an underlying note that everything should be split down the middle equally even if one of the two people is much more financially successful. You worry that if they knew your modest financial condition, they would judge you or stop dating you. You always have the feeling you're together but still on your own, a distinct "you have yours, and I have mine" vibe.

I'm not suggesting that one person pays for everything all the time. I'm not suggesting that healthy relationships comingle finances immediately. I'm suggesting that emotionally unavailable people have robust defense mechanisms when it comes to money and will make that clearly known.

8. **They are uncomfortable receiving or giving gifts.** It feels way too much like an actual relationship to get a gift from you. And they most certainly do not want to reciprocate. Even a small token of your affection can make them feel profoundly uncomfortable. They don't want to owe you anything.

9. **They say "thank you" after sex.** If after a ruckus roll in the hay your partner says, "thank you" like you just did

them a favor, the chances arc almost 100% that they are emotionally unavailable to you. They view the intimate act you just completed in a completely different way than you do.

You may view sex as fun but also as a way to connect, express love, and give pleasure to your partner. They may see sex as fun, pleasurable and on the same level as giving them ride home from the airport. A favor. They might only refer to sex as "f**king," because that is all it means to them.

Sex is fun, sex is pleasurable. In the context of an emotionally healthy relationship, sex is how you use your body to communicate how you feel about your partner. When you're together physically, you feel like they are in it for the sex but not in it for the sex with **you**.

10. **They distance themselves from intimacy as soon as sex is over.** It's pretty standard and typical for some people, especially men, to go to sleep right after sex. They're happy and exhausted. A lot of people might flip on the T.V., But an emotionally unavailable person is uncomfortable with intimacy and wants distance from it, and fast.

Right after sex, they might announce they have "some errands to do" and leave. You somehow find yourself heading to your car within a half hour after sex because they limit the amount of time you can be at their home by making excuses or double booking you.

There will always be a reasonable excuse why they have to go, or you have to leave but the hangout time after sex will be limited.

Even if they aren't quickly exiting you after sex there are other distancing behaviors that an emotionally unavailable person will employ to escape intimacy. They can become critical, pick a fight, or immediately start working on a project around the home or from work.

They may start talking about their past sexual partners or yours. They may ask about who else you would like to sleep with or celebrities you fantasize about, virtually inviting the thought of other people into the bed that you two were just sharing.

11. **They talk about how much they value their independence.** When an emotionally unavailable person says they value freedom and don't need a relationship, you might consider that they value their independence above being with you.

Emotionally healthy people do not curl up into a ball and die if they are not in a relationship, but they do have a desire, space in their life, that a relationship will fill.

Emotionally healthy, independent people don't need to grind their independence into the ground. They are okay on their own, but they do long for companionship. Emotionally unavailable people wear independence like a badge of honor. They value self-sufficiency above many other qualities.

They criticize their past partners for not being self-sufficient. They may also call you "too needy" when you're just trying to connect emotionally.

They react harshly or disappear any time they perceive you threaten their independence. It can be as simple as you want to date exclusively. Or when introducing your partner to someone, refer to them as your boyfriend or girlfriend, and you've been dating for months.

It's great to be independent and be able to take care of yourself. But emotionally unavailable men and women go a step further. They will proclaim things like "I don't need a man in my life to be happy." While that may be true, people who feel emotionally secure generally don't need to make grandiose statements to that effect. Typically, the emotionally unavailable person talks about their independence with such determination, you wonder who they are trying to convince.

12. **They avoid physical touch outside of bed.** Your partner won't hold your hand in public. In fact, they try to limit all contact when out in public. Lots of people don't like PDA, and that's fine. But if people assume that you are friends, cousins, or co-workers because they never see a single sign of affection, it's a message that your date is sending you. "I don't want other people to take our relationship seriously. I want to keep my options open."

If your partner continually walks ahead of you, they may be trying to create distance. They certainly aren't trying to keep the connection between you. Sure, you might have different walking paces naturally but walking ahead of you forms an invisible boundary that makes them feel comfortable. It also shows their lack of concern about you because you are on your own will need to take care of yourself.

13. **Social media silence.** You've been dating for months, and they don't friend you on social media or change their relationship status. They won't post a single picture of you together, or worse they'll post a great picture of you two together, but you're cropped out. They'll post a picture of a

fantastic view on a hike you just took but won't mention that the hike was with you.

14. **You do all the work.** Emotionally healthy relationships meet both partners' needs and are about give and take. If you're with an emotionally unavailable partner, you feel like you're doing the relationship completely their way and doing all the work to maintain it.

15. **They don't consider you in decision-making.** When making important decisions, they may think about how that decision impacts every person in their life except you. It doesn't even occur to them that their choices may affect you, because after all, it's not like you're in a relationship.

16. **They change.** Emotionally unavailable people often go from charming to chill. When you first met, they were fascinating, and let you know they wanted to be with you. They went from interested and engaged to not interested and disengaged.

Truthfully, sometimes in the course of dating, you find out that the other person isn't a good fit for you. An emotionally healthy person will recognize this and gently end things. An emotionally unavailable person may not stop seeing you, but they won't move the relationship forward either. They have changed from romantic partner to friends with or without benefits.

17. **Speaking about the relationship and your future.** When you are dating a passive emotionally unavailable person, you get the impression that your partner wants a relationship but just one that moves very slowly. You may think it is possible to have a future, but you're not 100% sure where you stand in their life and what their ultimate intentions are.

They avoid talking about your relationship in the future, always keeping things in the now. They become agitated if you bring up the future or any step towards commitment; even if that step is to let friends you both know that you're regularly dating.

Conversely an aggressive emotionally unavailable partner might seduce you on the first date, and start talking about moving in or your impending nuptials a week after you start dating. They come on as quickly as a tornado, wreck emotional havoc, and then spin off onto the next unsuspecting person.

18. **They avoid conflict or heart-to-heart talks in general.** Emotionally unavailable people want to keep everything emotionally light. Talking about how you feel, addressing your needs in a relationship or working through any conflict is something they seek to avoid. Being authentic and real can bring a couple closer

together, and closeness is precisely what they want to avoid.

19. **They view a formalized relationship and conflict as synonymous.** An emotionally unavailable person will see all attempts to communicate your needs, wants and desires within the relationship as conflict. They know that two adults have to work at maintaining a relationship and they don't want to do it.

20. **Their exes tell you they are emotionally unavailable.** A lot of what people say about their partner after they leave a relationship is untrue or born out of bitterness or anger. There were reasons your partner's prior relationships didn't work out.

It is a fallacy that it takes two to break a relationship. One person can break a relationship all on their own accord.

But if you find out that every single one of your partner's exes refers to them as controlling, demanding, a perfectionist, or emotionally checked out or unavailable, then you might step back and take a minute to consider whether it's smoke or actual fire.

21. **They are picky.** They have a constant attention to detail when it comes to you. You feel criticized or judged over things that don't matter. You may wonder what they're

going to point out about your appearance, your home, your car, your children, about the way you eat, the way you speak, or the way you interact socially every time you see them.

You feel like you're not sure if you measure up to their standard and don't feel like they will ultimately be accepting or gracious to you. We all evaluate our partners for compatibility. We all want to be with someone that we can respect, but emotionally unavailable people use extreme critiquing or judging as a distancing measure to talk themselves out of their romantic feelings toward you.

They feel the need to improve you or intentionally try to find things that are wrong with you so that they feel better about keeping their distance emotionally.

22. **They're hot and cold and hot and cold and hot and cold.** An emotionally unavailable partner will pull you close, and then push you away. After a fantastic date, you won't hear from them for several days. After intimate time spent together, they need to push back and rebalance their independence. One day you feel like the relationship is finally going somewhere and then they're gone. Closeness makes you feel good; proximity makes them want to run.

23. **I love you...NOT.** Saying I love you goes two different ways. They say it quickly, well before they have had time

to get to know you, much less love you. Or conversely, unless you say "I love you" first, and they say "I love you" in return you never hear it at all.

In fact, they may even tell you that they don't love you and never will. Ouch. But they still want to keep you around from time to time because it makes them feel good to be desired and even emotionally unavailable people like companionship and sex occasionally.

24. **You've gone from secure attachment to anxious attachment.** Most people who find themselves dating an emotionally unavailable person are emotionally unavailable themselves. However, once in a while an ordinarily secure person finds themselves in a dating relationship with someone who is emotionally unavailable.

Typically this happens when the emotionally unavailable person is the aggressive type who comes on strong at the beginning. So it takes a while for the secure person to figure it out. If you find yourself worried about where you stand in the relationship and are analyzing every text, email, or phone call that you get from them for signs they care about you because you're just not sure, it's time to think about what's driving that anxiety.

25. **Sexually you're in fast forward mode**. Lots of people have sex on the first date. No judgment here, but that's

what it is, sex. It is not possible to form a loving emotional attachment the first day you meet someone.

Lots of people believe in love at first sight, and I am not here to dissuade them because that can happen. But there are a lot of both males and females who are just looking for casual sex with no emotional attachment.

They'd like to date you and sleep with you, but they're never going to be your boyfriend or girlfriend. Sadly, some people feel that the only thing they can offer is sex. They use seduction to gloss over the fact they are unable to be emotionally intimate.

If your texts are more about sex than anything else, chances are you will never form a relationship, even if you end up living together. If you receive texts frequently late at night, it's also a warning sign of how they view you.

26. **Flattery will get you everywhere.** Some people have the gift of social charm. All of us have met genuinely charming, gracious people. It is perfectly reasonable to be on your best behavior and be complimentary when you're dating someone.

But at the beginning of the relationship, some emotionally unavailable people will pour on the charm, ever quick to compliment and never criticize.

They will be fascinated, captivated, infatuated, and engrossed in you. Except they've only just met you. An emotionally unavailable person can use flattery as a way to lower your defenses because it isn't you that they really want. Not every person who compliments you will be emotionally unavailable but be careful if that flattery comes on thick and fast.

27. **Complains about past relationships.** It's possible for one person to break up a relationship all by themselves. It's also possible to date or marry someone who is not a good fit or is abusive. However, when you discuss past relationships take note on whether their comments are mostly negative.

If the relationship failure was, "entirely the other person's fault" or they disparage their former partner vigorously, with anger or bitterness; this might be a red flag, because the person who is getting discredited next time maybe you.

When having discussions about past relationships, most people will talk about why the relationship failed. Most emotionally healthy people will make it clear what their part in the relationship failure was.

When having the "past relationship" talk, ask the other person what they learned from it. An emotionally healthy person will be able to answer that question.

Someone who avoids emotional intimacy will only speak about their former partner negatively or say something similar to this: "I learned never to date a crazy (insert a b**ch, b*st*rd, or whatever) again." They failed to learn anything about themselves or acknowledge their own responsibility.

If one person in the relationship is mostly to blame, there are ways that you are responsible too even if it was putting up with poor treatment from them and an emotionally healthy person knows that. We all make errors. Emotionally healthy people acknowledge their part of the mistakes and gain knowledge of how to operate at a higher level of emotional intelligence from their failures.

28. **Groundhog's Day.** Do you remember the movie Groundhog's Day? Bill Murray's character has to continually re-live that same day until he gets it right. Hand-in-hand with complaining about past partners and faulting them exclusively for the relationship failure, an emotionally unavailable person will describe past relationships, that while different, all seem the same.

They may describe every person they dated as crazy, or needy, or emotionally unstable. We all have a type. Until we learn to recognize why we choose a particular type of person to date, we might find ourselves repeatedly falling into the same trap. But an emotionally unavailable person is not able, or willing, to learn about themselves or to take personal responsibility for their feelings and change the type of long term partner they seek.

If the person you are dating seems like they've had a problem picking emotionally healthy people in every relationship they've had up to this point, you have to start wondering why they are interested in you.

29. **We're not trying to be devious, we'll tell you directly.** Many emotionally unavailable people are not evil; they are in it for something casual. They like to go on the occasional date or to have sex. Sometimes they need a regular person to attend work functions or other social events with, but they have no intention of having an actual relationship with you.

How do you know? They tell you. They say things like "I'm not ready for a relationship." "I can't ever imagine myself getting married again." "I like being independent." These same people can be fun, charming and engaging so what your hopeful self hears is "I haven't found the right one...yet."

Another lie we tell ourselves is that they need time to heal, to learn to trust, to be ready and we're the one that can help them trust again. We often think that the emotionally unavailable person *does* want a relationship because they are sending relationship signals, but that they are wary because they have been hurt.

It is so tempting to believe that we will be the person that they will trust and with whom they will want a relationship. But if a person tells you that they don't want anything serious, and you do, as painful as it is, you will need to move on.

30. **Underlying emotion and the treatment of others.** When you're in any dating relationship, it's important to note how the person you're with treats other people. Rude, denigrating behavior toward the wait staff is something to record as a red flag because it's wrong and may indicate later treatment of you.

The same thing is true of how they speak about their family. Conflict and turmoil within the greater family unit and how they speak about them should be a sign that not all is well.

Conversely, people who show no emotion at all towards others can be a red flag as well. In a situation where an emotionally healthy person might feel embarrassed, an emotionally unavailable person might not express emotion at all.

If you're on a date and a waiter accidentally spills a glass of wine in the lap of your dating partner, they will probably express some emotion and hopefully good-humouredly laugh it off. An emotionally unavailable person may pretend it never happened because they avoid conflict, or awkwardness, or embarrassment at any cost. They will cringe if you bring the incident up even in a gentle, teasing way.

31. **Their ego.** Emotionally unavailable people tend to swing with the pendulum with regard to their ego. They either spend a lot of time telling you how great they are, how successful, how wise, and how much money or stuff they have, or they swing the other way entirely.

    Some emotionally unavailable people tend toward low goals in life. They are humble, but so much so they've abdicated all responsibility of taking care of themselves.

    Emotionally healthy people don't brag too much, nor do they self-deprecate too much, they're just comfortable with themselves and able to be satisfied with you whether you have as much success or worldly possessions as they have.

32. **The inner critic, the outer perfectionist:** Show me a perfectionist, and I will show you a person with a scathing inner critic. If you think being in a relationship with the perfectionist is hard work, you ought to try to spend a day

in their head. Perfectionists live in fear of being rejected so they are always on the lookout for anything that might lead to being rejected.

Both perfectionism and OCD are emotionally debilitating not just for the relationship but the person suffering from them. Their fear of rejection is the root of their fear of intimacy, and the reality is that they are going to evaluate you with the same standard of perfection as a way to self-protect from your rejection. Perfectionists don't just look at something; they focus on their perception of the why behind something.

Having a heart surgeon that is a perfectionist is a good thing. Being in a relationship with someone who is going to point out every little flaw and interrogate you, albeit gently about the hidden meaning behind every small flaw is exhausting.

Finding things wrong with you is a distancing mechanism so that if the relationship fails they can feel good that they dodged the bullet rather than take responsibility for themselves. You cannot please a perfectionist or someone who highly values appearance.

33. **Either I'm in charge, or you're in charge.** There are two sides to controlling a relationship when it comes to dating an emotionally unavailable person. If they are an

aggressive emotionally unavailable person, they want the relationship to revolve around them. You will be subject to their timing or pace of how things progress. They will not inconvenience or change their schedule to suit you. They will not make any changes in their life to accommodate you.

The flip side of that coin is a passive emotionally unavailable person who will make you entirely in charge of the relationship. An aggressive emotionally unavailable person wants everything on their terms and is typically labeled a commitment-phobic person. A passive emotionally unavailable person can commit but they are usually passive aggressive in relationship development.

34. **Working for the weekend.** One sign you're dating someone who is emotionally unavailable is that you hear from your dating partner during the week, but there is no attempt to make weekend plans with you. That is because they have a life that doesn't include you and isn't going to include you anytime in the future.

35. **You do not know their friends.** If after three months you haven't met the friends of the person you're dating, your relationship isn't going anywhere beyond casual dating. Most people evaluate the person they are dating

and decide within the first six weeks about whether you genuinely are relationship material.

Sometimes due to circumstances beyond control, it can take a while to start to meet your new partner's friends. But if after three months you don't know who they are and they haven't met yours, you may need to reevaluate whether you have a relationship.

36. **They have feelings...just not for you.** Sometimes people are emotionally unavailable for the right reasons. When someone is recovering from a break-up, they are temporarily emotionally unavailable. There is no possibility that someone whose heart is full of pain, anger, and grief has any room in it to have space for you.

When people go through a break-up, they miss the emotional connection of being with someone. Often they seek out a new relationship to fill the void, to ease the pain, because they want sex, and to soothe their ego. They want reassurance that they are still desirable. Unfortunately, they're in the dating relationship to get all their needs met and really have nothing to give back.

Everyone who goes through a break-up is temporarily emotionally unavailable because they need to heal. There are a small amount of people who go on to marry the first person they date after going through a break-up, but most people do not. Most rebound relationships are temporary. Try not to let yourself be the rebound relationship because it hurts. Wait for the person to heal before dating them; you'll be glad you did.

Chapter Four:
The Committers: Signs You May Be in A Relationship with an Emotionally Unavailable Person.

Signs you are married or in a long term relationship with an emotionally unavailable person:

A lot of the information available on the internet on the emotionally unavailable person is exclusively about the dating or early relationship phase. And that's unfortunate, because millions of people are living in a loveless, sexless marriage or long term relationship and are desperate to fix it and don't even know where to begin.

Many people reading this book will be married or in a committed relationship and wondering if they can make it to the ten year mark. Or maybe you were like Abby, nineteen years and wondering can you make it twenty?

The process of being emotionally unavailable isn't one-dimensional. Most people don't wake up one morning and tell themselves "today is the day I am going to emotionally shut down for the rest of my life."

It's a lifelong commitment to the protection of defense mechanisms, and those defense mechanisms can change as you age. The way an emotionally unavailable person acts during the dating phase can be different than the way they operate in a long-term relationship.

An emotionally unavailable person is capable of having sex during the dating phase of the relationship and withholding sex for emotional reasons during the marriage or long-term period of the relationship.

It's no surprise that people act differently as a relationship evolves. You hear people say, "He changed" or "She changed" and it's true. Hopefully, that change is for the better.

In most failed marriages there were warning signs during the dating phase that had there been an awareness of, would have resulted in the end of the relationship before it progressed to marriage or moving in. Some things were accepted or excused that may have bothered the emotionally healthy partner.

Typically, people who become involved with an emotionally unavailable person are very self-critical, have an anxious attachment style, and give a pass to the other person's behavior in ways they would never accept of their own behavior.

It is this very accepting nature that draws the emotionally unavailable person to them. They fear being rejected almost as a primal fear. Their perception of your acceptance is very intoxicating to them.

It's imperative to identify the signs of emotional unavailability and to address those issues at the beginning of the relationship, if they can be resolved.

For that reason, I'm happy that relationship blogs focus on that area. Unfortunately, many people find themselves in a long-term relationship with an emotionally unavailable partner and they may not have, or want, the option of ending the relationship.

Jim's ex-wife's emotional unavailability became much more pronounced after marrying almost to the point where he felt lied to about who Sheila represented herself to be when he married her. It was like an emotional switch flipped the moment the chase was over. The emotional unavailability gloves came off almost immediately after they said: "I do."

It's essential to denote that while there are commonalities there also can be differences in the way that an emotionally unavailable person acts during the short-term and long-term phases of the relationship.

After the marriage, things slowly shift. We all know about the honeymoon phase of relationships. In healthy relationships after the honeymoon period is over it feels like two people are attempting to row the boat together to the other shore. Sometimes the water is calm, and sometimes it's choppy, making the rowing a bit harder.

In an unhealthy long-term relationship with an unemotionally available partner, it feels like the other person is sitting there watching you row the boat by yourself to the other shore.

It becomes increasingly lonely and frustrating to go it alone. You beg them to do their part of the work; you put the oar in their hands to make it easier for them to row. You stop rowing too, but they will not do their part of the work on the relationship to get it to the other side. They don't care if the relationship boat drifts, as long as they don't have to be the one rowing.

And then a choice will be made. You abandon ship, or you accept that your partner will force you to do all the work of a relationship and on those terms, you stick it out and make it to the other side.

And that is why we must note the differences between signs you're dating someone who may be emotionally unavailable and how to identify that you are currently in a long-term relationship with someone who may be emotionally unavailable.

It would better not to get into a rowboat with someone you know is going to make you do all the rowing. Sometimes we don't know until the boat has left the dock that the other person has no intention of rowing. But if you're a person reading this that is already in the boat, in the middle of the lake, rowing furiously all by yourself, there is hope for you too.

As mentioned in the previous chapter, when trying to define the behaviors that characterize an emotionally unavailable person it's also important to understand that emotional unavailability has both passive and aggressive characteristics.

An emotionally unavailable person might be entirely passive and display passive behaviors altogether in the long term relationship. They may also be wholly aggressive and exhibit only aggressive emotional behaviors. Or they may be a combination and able to demonstrate both types of reactions within the relationship.

I point this out to you because a list of the characteristics of a relationship with an emotionally unavailable person may seem a little bipolar. That's because you or the person you care about may either be a passive emotionally unavailable person or an aggressive emotionally unavailable person.

For eleven years Sandy was married to a passive emotionally unavailable person. Someone who chose shut down emotionally unless she specifically addressed his behavior in the relationship and then he would immediately shift to an aggressive posture becoming extremely angry.

We all have a fight or flight tendency. Sandy's ex-husband's pattern was flight, flight, flight unless confronted on his behavior and then it was a sudden shift to fight. She learned that she could approach him about his emotional unavailability, but there would be an immediate price to pay in the form of rage.

It is possible to be a passive emotionally unavailable person or an aggressive emotionally unavailable person or flex back and forth between both. The critical key in all of it, the root of the problem is a singular unwillingness, a commitment, to never be hurt emotionally or made to feel uncomfortable.

Here are some signs of being in a long-term relationship with an emotionally unavailable partner you can trust, keeping in mind some are passive, and some are aggressive:

1. **They avoid conflict.**

The instant a disagreement begins, no matter how mild; a passive emotionally unavailable person will get an expression on their face denoting a child who is receiving a reprimand. They want to end the discussion as soon as possible. They let you say how you feel, but they won't or are unable to say how they feel in return.

They immediately agree to make a change, but their actions never actually change. The conversation seems closer to parent correcting a child than an adult negotiating with an adult.

You find yourself thinking of ways to make the solution to the problem easier on them. At the end of the discussion, you feel sorry for them and regret bringing it up. Or worse yet, you feel like a jerk for mentioning your needs, and that's the real problem.

Another area of conflict avoidance for the passive emotionally unavailable person is the unwillingness to state needs, wants, desires or irritations. Instead, they may behave in a very passive aggressive way or become "quietly angry."

It is clear that they are irritated, something is not right, but it will feel too much like a conflict to talk about what is bothering them.

An emotionally healthy person would be able to say, "When you use my car keys, please put them back where you found them, so I don't have to look for them when I need them because being late for work is super stressful to me," without viewing it as a potential major conflict or criticism.

The passive emotionally unavailable person will feel that irritation but will never tell you, instead internalizing it as another brick in the emotional wall. They won't seem quite right, but you're not sure what you've done. Often they will withdraw and ignore you.

The aggressive emotionally unavailable person may yell or throw the keys expressing emotion that is an overreaction to the situation.

Conflict is either avoided or managed emotionally, either way, they will view it as another way that you are inferior to them.

2. **You are to blame.**

It is an inexplicable truth that the emotionally unavailable person views their partner as both inferior and superior to them simultaneously.

There is no way to overcome this paradox because ultimately it means **your partner views you, not them, as the problem.** And if you don't learn anything else from this book, please take a moment to consider that.

Whether you're reading this book because you believe yourself to be emotionally unavailable or the person you love is emotionally unavailable the fact remains that emotionally unavailable people are avoiding the blame because it is emotionally scary to accept responsibility.

The foundation of emotional health is to be responsible for yourself and view yourself, not others, as your own most significant problem. Other people influence us, but ultimately we alone have the power to decide how we feel, react, and think.

The beliefs we have about ourselves impact us far more significantly than any action taken by another human being. If you've been a victim of a violent crime, or abuse of any type that might be a hard concept to accept. I encourage you to allow yourself a little room to think about whether it's true. What someone does to us is their part, what we think about ourselves in response to their actions is our part.

The reason an emotionally unavailable person avoids conflict is a direct result of the way they feel about themselves. It is much easier to make you the problem then work with themselves to overcome their own pain and fear. They do not take responsibility for how they feel. They feel if they do it will confirm the very pain they are trying to avoid.

They can become internally overly critical of you as a way to feel better about themselves. People aren't evil for doing this. It's a common defense mechanism or reaction to conflict that most people use. Passive emotionally unavailable people take it to the next level.

Have you ever almost gotten into a car accident with another vehicle and immediately expressed anger and blamed the other driver? That fear, that reaction of rage, the impetus to immediately believe the other party was trying to hurt you intentionally, is what emotionally unavailable people feel when you do something, even accidentally, that hits their fear or pain spot.

Since they don't want to feel threatened and are unable or unwilling to address the emotions that arise and the fear behind those emotions they often shut down and blame you.

When this happens, you may feel hurt, criticized, misjudged and blamed. Since you cannot get your partner to address the conflict directly, people often resort to getting louder to get heard by yelling, name calling or being overly hurtful when trying to communicate your feelings. And when you do that in response to passive-aggressive behavior, you not only confirm the conflict the emotionally unavailable person is seeking to avoid, you justify their belief that they are superior to you and you are the problem.

3. **Ghosts.**

The emotionally unavailable person is there and yet not there. Have you ever ridden the haunted house ride at Disneyland? Near the end of the ride, your cart flips around to face a mirror. A ghost appears to be riding in the buggy right next to you. They are there, but not there.

An emotionally unavailable person may be physically present in the room but will only respond when asked a direct question. They might laugh at a funny comment, but they will not contribute or engage in the conversation in any meaningful way. They will do the least possible they can to be present whether at the regular evening meal or time spent with extended family.

Being an emotional parasite is one way of describing a continuously checked-out person. The emotionally unavailable person will always depend on you to do the heavy emotional communication. They will vicariously be experiencing emotion and connection through you.

The emotionally unavailable person will always expect you to be the one who maintains the relationship with family and friends. They will not engage, initiate or put themselves out of their comfort zone in any family gathering. They hold themselves closed, revealing nothing. They can, and often will, spend an entire family event saying nothing at all unless someone is directly speaking to them.

The passive emotionally unavailable person can make an introvert look like an extrovert in comparison. In fact, they often use the excuse of being an introvert to justify their checked-out behavior. Introverts are people who emotionally replenish when being alone. That does not mean that they are unable to interact socially. Being introverted doesn't mean being antisocial, it means a little downtime after a big social event to re-center yourself.

It is possible for people to be shy especially in the first few contacts with others. Many people suffer social anxiety in large groups. But the emotionally unavailable person maintains their closed-off behavior and lack of interaction well beyond what would be considered reasonable to become comfortable with your family or friends. And it isn't shyness or anxiety that is causing them to close off; it's a decision that they are not going to exert the effort of interaction.

You go to dinner with your family. During dinner, everyone participates in the conversation except your emotionally unavailable partner. They seem to have a good time, they laugh at the jokes and respond albeit briefly, when asked a specific question directed at them. They are there sitting at the table during dinner, but they are not present.

After dinner, you asked if anything's wrong. You gently mention that they were very quiet and that you would love for your family to get to know them the same way you do. Your partner swiftly agrees but at the next family gathering, and the next one, and the one after that it is the same. They are there physically, but that's about it.

When with your family, you find yourself trying harder and harder to engage your partner in the conversation. You might even make arrangements with your family that you think will individually engage your partner. You may make excuses to your family like your partner is not feeling well, or has a headache, or is tired from work to explain their lack of engagement or interaction.

You find yourself performing relationship gymnastics trying to foster a connection. Three years later the only thing your family knows about your significant other has been learned from you because your partner has barely spoken to them. There has been zero effort on their part to build any relationship with your family or friends despite repeated opportunities to do so.

And it's not just your family. The ghost or emotional parasite may rely on you to take over the relationship with their family as well. They don't have to expend the effort of emotional engagement when they have you to do it for them. Abdication of family contact can be especially true if a large part of the reason why your partner is emotionally unavailable is rooted in their childhood.

In some ways, you feel like the unspoken go-between in every meaningful relationship your emotionally unavailable partner has whether that is with your children or family and friends.

4. **A decisive lack of decision-making.**

A passive emotionally unavailable partner never wants to decide if they can help it. They never want to be the bad guy. They avoid rejection by never giving you an opportunity to reject them for a decision they've made. Their mantra is, "That sounds like a decision for you."

It can be as simple as never picking the restaurant you are going to eat at. They might go on the vacation, possibly, but they certainly aren't going to plan it. They have no opinion on most things and if they do have an opinion they can to keep it to themselves. They deviate from this only slightly when they slide into a subtle criticism of you.

You find yourself pretending they're going to help make a decision. You present all the options to them. But they ultimately defer to you.

Great news! You're almost always going to get your way when your partner is passively emotionally unavailable.

The bad news? There is a price to pay. Since you make all the decisions, you are responsible for everything. And if, despite your best efforts, anything goes wrong it's your fault because after all, you are the one who made the decision.

It is a tempting trap because in the beginning there are no conflicts. Your opinion is highly valued, and that seems nice. But the shine soon wears off. Being the only decision-maker in the relationship is a heavy burden to bear.

It means that you will be the only one to discipline the children. Unless of course the kid's behavior somehow hits the fear or pain button in which case disproportionate discipline based on anger is likely to happen. And guess who gets to fix that?

It means that you have the responsibility for the finances. If there is ever a time in your life where you financially struggle you will have to come up with all the solutions, and you will be the one to blame.

It means you will never feel protected by your partner. Since in general, they blame you and they typically take the other person's side. If they didn't, they would have to come up with a solution to the problem and, after all, isn't that your department as the decision-maker?

It means you might not only get labeled, but actually called controlling. Not just by your emotionally unavailable partner but by family and friends.

Because it doesn't occur to the people judging you that your partner may steadfastly refuse to make any decisions, be the bad guy, participate in the parenting or do anything that they perceive associated with conflict.

You make all the decisions because you are forced to make all the decisions.

The problem isn't your willingness to allow your partner to step up. The problem isn't that you are controlling. The problem isn't that you insist on everything your way. The problem is your partner doesn't want any part of the responsibility. They are so afraid of doing something wrong and being judged for it that while being physically and intellectually able, they can be entirely emotionally incapable of making a decision.

There are millions of people who feel completely alone even though they are in a relationship and if you are one of them I understand how that hurts and I'm sorry.

5. Childish behavior.

Boys who never want to grow up, girls who are always the baby. Lots of people enjoy video games, TV, shopping and sports. But an emotionally unavailable person never seems to want to grow up. They may spend hours avoiding relationship by playing video games, or watching sports or going shopping.

Are you tempted to call the computer your partner's "mistress?" Does your partner play an extraordinary amount of video games? The reality is that your partner may not want to be in the relationship and is using the computer as a passive way to be in the relationship but not be present in the relationship. They may not want to break up, but they may not want to stay together either. They may want to able to have a partner, two children, and a house with a white picket fence without ever having to grow up past their teenage video game phase.

They may agree to a budget but avoid conflict about overspending. They can be an emotional child in an adult's body. When you attempt to speak to your partner about finances, some use baby talk, or pouting, or sex to avoid dealing with the real issue. They can throw tantrums and blame you as if the problem wasn't overspending, but you aren't earning enough money or taking good enough care of them.

6. The won't protect you.

An emotionally unavailable partner cannot protect you because to do so they would have to engage in conflict and make you the first priority in their social life. They won't stand up for you to their family or friends. They won't be there for you if somebody is rude to you or attacks you. You are on your own. If someone criticizes you whether publicly or privately, they will not defend you.

They will politely listen to the other party and remain neutral or, worse yet, take the other side to please the complaining person and end the conflict. The emotionally unavailable partner is unable to have empathy for you. When you are hurt and explain your side of the situation or conflict they immediately default to playing the devil's advocate which is an incredibly unloving thing to do.

In every conversation with them about a conflict, they immediately take the other person's side. Instead of sharing your feelings with them, you end up in the exhausting position of defending yourself. What could've been a moment of comfort and understanding turns into a discussion about how you can improve. You leave the conversation feeling misunderstood and second-guessing yourself rather than being loved and accepted.

7. Separate vacations.

When you are married to them, an emotionally unavailable partner may not want to go on vacation with you or want to take separate vacations. In healthy relationships, lots of people plan and take "guys only" or "girls only" time. But some emotionally unavailable people will not go on vacation with you or your family. There is value in connection and shared experiences when you spend time together away. The emotionally unavailable person doesn't want that connection and may even feel overwhelmed by the thought of that much time away with you.

8. **Anger.**

Many people get angry in reaction to injustice, but their anger is disproportionate. An emotionally unavailable person will use anger to build a defensive wall around them. They may express anger in many ways such as yelling, rage, throwing things, hitting things, or other types of loss of control. Silence, sarcasm, angry tone, biting remarks, criticism, and name-calling are also used to convey displeasure. They can be unnecessarily cruel.

9. **Sex or lack thereof.**

Many marriages are sexless, meaning having sex less than ten times a year. If you are in a relationship with an emotionally unavailable person, the number of times you were intimate in a given year may be a lot less than ten.

It's very common in healthy relationships for the partners to have different amounts of sexual desire and need for frequency. Most healthy relationships include periods of time during pregnancy, illness or work stress where they take a break from sex.

A physical relationship with your partner is critical to maintaining intimacy. If one person in the relationship withdraws emotionally, they will not want to experience that intimacy. A sexless relationship is a visible sign that one or both of the partners is withdrawing emotionally and the relationship needs help, or it will be doomed to fail.

10. **On the defense.**

Every relationship hits the occasional snag, and things come up. In an emotionally healthy relationship, the parties work to have open, blame-free communication. But an emotionally unavailable partner does not have the emotional capacity to separate valid concerns, from attack.

An emotionally unavailable person might become defensive, suggesting you were attacking them, or are never satisfied, or that you are a nag.

They might feel unreasonably scolded. They may lash back in anger or display a defensive behavior such as immediately pointing out your flaws, even if what you're trying to discuss is reasonable and presented in a calm, non-judgmental manner.

Another way an emotionally unavailable person may handle a discussion of an issue is to withdraw by becoming complicit.

They listen to you as if they agree but offer no input of their own. Although they say nothing, they do not agree with you and have no intention of changing their behavior or complying with your reasonable request. They want the conversation to be over as quickly as possible, and acquiescence is the fastest way to make that happen. To them, the problem isn't the actual issue; it's your pointing out there is an issue that is a real problem.

11. **An emotional affair.** It seems ironic that someone who withdraws emotionally from the person they supposedly love and are in a committed relationship with can invest emotional energy in someone else.

When people have emotional affairs, they aren't connecting with the other person intimately they are merely expressing their emotions in a way that feels safe for them.

There isn't any emotional risk to them because the other person isn't even really involved, just the idea of them is. This doesn't make the fact that your significant other is having an emotional affair any less painful to you. The fantasy of the other person is a wall between you and no less real in an emotional sense than having an actual affair.

12. **Do they know you?** After years of marriage, your partner doesn't remember simple things about you. They

couldn't name your favorite color, your favorite type of food, or things you dislike.

Since they spend a lot of time in a dissociative state, physically but not emotionally present, they often don't notice your preferences. Do you hate chocolate, or are allergic to bee stings and despite you mentioning it several times your partner can't seem to remember?

You find yourself starting to wonder if they are incompetent because they continuously order you the wrong coffee or sandwich. It isn't a lack of brain power; it's a lack of being present. They can't remember your preferences because when you said it and repeated yourself over and over, they were inside their head and tuned you out.

Emotionally unavailable people can check out for long periods of time. They have mastered the habit of being in a room physically while their mind is far, far away.

13. **Pornography addiction**. If your partner is addicted to pornography than it is almost a certainty they have emotional intimacy connection issues. Porn has become the norm in our society. You can't look at any magazine, social media site or internet news outlet without seeing pictures of naked people.

Celebrities, Instagram stars, and most ads, in general, are sensuality based. Culturally we've seen desensitization to pornography in our daily life. It's very common for most people to see some form of nudity in images daily. Show me a person who hasn't seen Kim Kardashian's bare butt or breasts at least once in the last month, and I will show you someone who's living entirely off the grid.

While most people see some pornography daily, not everyone develops a fantasy life where fake intimacy is replacing real intimacy. It's challenging for the partner of a pornography addict not to feel rejected. Even if you understand that they are expressing intimacy in a way that feels safe to them, the fact remains they are refusing intimacy with you.

A partner's pornography addiction typically has nothing to do with your sexual performance or physical appearance. It's just a way for them to get gratification without paying the high price of intimacy. That doesn't make it less hurtful. In some relationships, pornography addiction can occur if one partner continually refuses sex. Pornography addictions can sometimes but not necessarily, indicate that there is more than one person in the relationship that is emotionally unavailable.

Lots of people look at pornography. Emotionally unavailable people take it a step further by using it to replace intimacy that they could have if they were willing to connect emotionally and risk being vulnerable with their partner.

14. **They have a substance abuse problem**. If your partner has an addiction to alcohol, illegal drugs, prescription medication, or the newly legalized marijuana they are almost certainly emotionally unavailable.

While it is true many intoxicated people lower their defense mechanisms and say what they really think when they are inebriated we can all agree if you need to have a shot of whiskey or smoke a joint to be able to talk about your feelings or say what you really mean, you have a problem.

While your partner may be able to say what they think under the influence, they aren't going to be able to connect or change. It is not possible to be emotionally available and addicted at the same time. Most people who struggle with substance abuse do so because they are trying to avoid how they feel inside.

Even those predisposed with genetic addiction tendencies cannot work through emotional unavailability while they are using. If your partner has a substance abuse problem, addressing it is essential before a genuine emotional connection can take place.

15. **They struggle with depression.** Has anyone ever asked you to borrow money, even a small amount which you would have given willingly had you had any cash on you at all?

As much as they may want to, depressed people cannot give what they do not possess.

Sometimes emotional unavailability has nothing to do with you, the state of your relationship, or their desire to connect emotionally. Depression can rob a person of their ability to risk emotional connection, and they are powerless to stop it. Many people who struggle with depression report that they feel held hostage by sadness. This type of emotional unavailability still impacts you, but it is generally solvable because it isn't a choice, it's a temporary, treatable condition. Get to a doctor, and do it now!

The list of signs that you are dating or in a long-term relationship with an emotionally available partner is not exhaustive. But if you have had experiences or recognize your partner or yourself in many of these examples, then you probably need some healing in yourself, your partner and your relationship. And here's the good news: it is possible for an emotionally detached person to heal and to become someone who can experience an emotional connection. Read on to part two!

PART TWO
The Solution.

Chapter Five:
The Change Possibility: Can an Emotionally Unavailable Person Become Emotionally Available?

Can an emotionally unavailable person become emotionally available? Yes, emotional unavailability does not have to be a relationship death sentence. It is possible to overcome.

Most advice given to people who are involved with an emotionally unavailable person is to leave the relationship; dump and run as fast as you can. That might be the right advice, especially if your partner has been presented the opportunity to change over and over but wants the relationship to remain as it is, without any change on their part.

It's possible that ending the relationship might be the wrong advice. How does abandoning the relationship help someone who wants to become emotionally available but doesn't know how?

Being emotionally unavailable is a choice, conditioning, a reaction, in response to pain and fear. Recognizing the roots, addressing the pain, and dealing with your anxiety can help you to become emotionally healthy.

People become emotionally unavailable because it feels safer. It is a coping mechanism. Emotional unavailability isn't about being unable to express emotions. Emotionally unavailable people can be angry, bitter, jealous, happy, and calm. They can experience and project a variety of emotions. What they are not able to do is allow themselves to be fully open, to risk personal rejection.   .

And it is all about risk. Imagine two people are offered the same stock to buy from their broker. It's a very high-risk stock but also has an unbelievably fantastic return. The buy-in is $1000.   One person has $1000 to invest; the other has $10,000 to invest. When the first investor buys one issue of stock, at $1000. he risks losing all he has. When the investor with $10,000 buys one issue of stock, he's risking $1,000. If the stock goes bad, he still has $9,000 left in the bank. Which investor do you think would be willing to risk more? The person who would lose it all or the person who would still have 90% of his investment funds left intact if the stock should go belly up?

Emotionally unavailable people have lower risk tolerance and a very high level of self-protection. They have a limited amount to invest. If they lose, what do they have left? To become emotionally available, you need to build your emotional bank account so that you can risk opening yourself up to both love and pain.

Overcoming emotional unavailability can be achieved when a person is willing to learn what specific fears are holding them back from being a fully open person. A lack of awareness, self-compassion, defense mechanisms, and reactions from their partner all play their part in closing the emotionally unavailable person off.

There is no instant cure for emotional unavailability. None of us can be spontaneously self-aware, filled with self-compassion or lay our defense mechanisms down but we can commit to work with ourselves and build up a relationship risk tolerance.

In the following chapters I highlight fours areas in your life that you can work on to increase your emotional intelligence capacity and move toward being a secure healthy person.

Chapter Six:
Becoming Emotionally Aware.

"The first step is awareness" is an overused phrase that is entirely true and yet devoid of any real help or meaning. Awareness isn't recognizing that you have a problem, its taking responsibility for a problem you have.

There is a reason why Alcoholics Anonymous asks participants to begin speaking by introducing themselves this way: "my name is _____, and I am an alcoholic." Emotionally unavailable people need to go beyond admitting they have a problem and realize they *ARE* the problem.

The basis of relational, emotional unavailability is self-protection from pain, either emotional or financial.

The basis of self-protection is that the other person or the relationship is the problem.

Emotional unavailability = "you might hurt me." You are the problem.

Emotional health = "I might get hurt." I take responsibility for myself.

The relationship, the other person, financial pressures, family issues, are not the problem. You are your own most significant problem, and that is true for everyone. Everyone risks getting hurt in a relationship. It is what you believe and the choices you go on to make as a result of that hurt ultimately impact your life the most.

Fear is like a pebble dropped into a lake that causes ripples in the otherwise calm surface. Once you release the stone, it's gone. What you see after the pebble disappears is the displaced energy.

Traumatic childhood events can elicit strong emotional reactions well into adulthood. Victims of abuse or neglect can experience emotional triggers in their everyday adult life.

When Stephanie was seven, she was coming home from a neighborhood park with a group of children when the little girl who was right behind her was struck and killed by a car that entered the intersection after the children had stepped into the crosswalk.

Stephanie becomes angry when she sees parents crossing the street with their young children too far away from them to protect them if needed. The problem isn't that the children are in danger or that she has an anger issue.

The problem is that she experiences pain related to a past traumatic event, which elicits fear, which then is expressed by a reaction of anger.

And then she has a choice to makc, bccause you manage your mania or it manages you.

She can:

-Yell at the parents. (reaction of aggression)

-Run and assist children in crossing the street. (A reaction of managing.)

-She can alert everyone to the danger. (A reaction of hyper-vigilance to a perceived threat.)

-She can attempt to fix the parents. (A reaction of perfectionism.)

Or

She can realize that pain from the past event is surfacing and deal with that.

In general, Stephanie does believe parents ought to always try to keep their children safe and well supervised. But in this situation, she is experiencing fear and pain based on her perception of what might happen. She can either blow up and withdraw or acknowledge that losing her friend at such a young age was scary, hurtful and that she is hyper-vigilant or overprotective in trying to avoid dealing with those feelings. She could realize that she had no control over her friend dying and as a six-year-old, it was not her responsibility to keep everyone safe. She could forgive the adults in the situation and most importantly, herself.

Awareness isn't experiencing the emotions; it is making a decision about what you do with them, that matters. It's what you then believe about yourself and others to be true that damages you. For many, it isn't the actual divorce or break-up that hurts as much as thinking that they are not worth loving and the sense of rejection and failure that does the lasting damage. Awareness concerning a relationship and emotional unavailability means:

1. You recognize you have feelings of fear and pain related to past experiences.

2. You acknowledge that you have reactions and make decisions based on those feelings.

3. You understand that it is your reactions, resulting beliefs and decisions that will impact you far more significantly than the other person's actions ever could.

4. You stop blaming the other person and acknowledge that you, not the other person, are your biggest problem.

5. You acknowledge your feelings, forgive yourself and others. You accept that people generally do the best they can with the tools they have at the time and let go.

6. You stop making decisions to believe lies based on fear and pain like "everyone will leave me" or "I'm flawed, broken and no one will ever be able to love me" or "I'll never have a great relationship."

Ways to practice and work with yourself on awareness:

1. Ask yourself "What" Questions

Take some time to analyze the situation the next time you experience anger, fear, or stress and ask yourself:

"What about that situation caused me to react negatively?"

"What about that situation caused me to think I needed to defend myself or others?"

"What about my relationship or interaction with that person causes me to be uncomfortable or afraid?"

"What event in my past might I unknowingly be linking this to?"

2. What is driving your behavior?

Write a personal timeline listing the most influential experiences both negative and positive, you've had in your life on blank paper in the landscape position. Draw a line on the middle of the page for the timeline. Write positive experiences above the line and negative experiences below the line. Draw a heart monitor like graph line from point to point. Study the pattern of your life.

What or who influenced you?

-Ask yourself, what you felt about each event on the timeline. Write those feelings under each item.

-Ask yourself what fears, anger, and pain are still influencing your current relationships?

-If you attach shame to any of the items on your timeline, make amends or let go and forgive yourself.

-Allow yourself to grieve. We all have things in our life that are unfair and wrong. Some of those instances could have been very influential in developing emotional unavailability. Acknowledge that they were wrong and you are worth being loved, cared for and treated better. Let go of the pain from those events.

3. Reflect on reactions.

Awareness doesn't happen overnight. At the beginning of the process, realization takes place AFTER the adverse event and subsequent reactions occur. Once you have had time to reflect rather than react, think about the interaction.

Don't beat on yourself for being closed or reacting but do work to take control of your emotions. The goal is not to become perfect but to learn why you react negatively and move forward toward openness. The next time you get upset, experience fear, irritation, or frustration ask yourself what's really going on. Try to figure out what exactly it is that is triggering your pain reaction.

4. Tell yourself the truth about your current relationship.

-Are you with someone who is going to hurt you, or not? If yes, end the relationship now. If the answer is no, give the relationship a chance.

-Does your partner allow him or herself to be loved and love back? If the answer is yes, recommit to making the relationship work. Acknowledge that how you feel about yourself is not your partner's fault. Take responsibility for your feelings and the way you view yourself.

5. Get help if needed.

Enter counseling or work with a Life Coach who specializes in emotional availability. This is especially critical if your timeline involves more negative influences than positive in your childhood. There are self-help groups for co-dependence.

Chapter Seven:
Learning to Practice Self-Compassion.

In the last chapter, we learned to give ourselves a good, hard look and if you're honest with yourself to be able to accept that internally things aren't looking so good. The emotionally unavailable person is going to have to face some things that make him or her uncomfortable. Since pain, self-loathing, perfectionism (phobia of being judged) or fear of abandonment is at the root of emotional unavailability, people need to practice self-compassion.

A relationship partner that lets the emotionally unavailable partner continue their behavior unchecked in the name of compassion is counter-productive and even damaging. You can't demand an emotionally unavailable person to change, nor can you accept the unloving behavior.

Since deep down they are unable to either trust or care for their partner (whether they're married to them or not), an excess of compassion from their partner isn't helpful, but gentle accountability is.

Self-compassion doesn't mean you justify your behavior, it means you begin to deal with your inner critical voice and your self-worth.

The root of emotional unavailability is not feeling worth being loved and fear of abandonment which expresses itself in either an arrogant or self-loathing way.

There are three main parts of the brain: the cerebrum, cerebellum, and brainstem.

The largest part of the brain, composed of right and left hemispheres, is called the cerebrum. It performs elevated functions like interpreting sight, touch, and sound, as well as reasoning, emotions, learning, and speech.

In the reason and emotion area, a lot is happening at once. When interpreting a situation, we make assumptions, have thoughts, and exhibit reactions simultaneously. Those thoughts are an acumination of both what is happening presently and what has happened in the past. We develop thought patterns which we refer to as our "inner voice."

Most people have a thought pattern or an inner voice directly related to things we *"should"* do. An expert at guilt, our "should" voice is trying to help us but does so in a very negative way. I *should* do my taxes, I *should* eat more healthy, I *should* do that chore I know I need to do, I *should* call my mom, I *should* say sorry even though the other person is wrong, I *should* exercise, I *should* laugh at my bosses' jokes even though they make me feel uncomfortable. You might also note that the word "need" is often interchangeable for the word should with the same connotation.

And along with the nagging "should" or "need to" demand is the promise of disaster if we do not obey. We conjure up an unpleasant scenario attached to whatever action we ought to take.

"You should (need to) take out the trash before she starts nagging you about it."

"You should (need to) say sorry and get it over with before this becomes a big fight."

"You should (need to) call your mom because if she dies, you'll feel terrible you didn't speak to her when you could have."

"You should (need to) lose weight because you look terrible and no one will ever be attracted to fat you."

"You should (need to) stop.... insert whatever perceived behavior is receiving bullying judgment by someone else.

We don't shut our "should" voice down because sometimes there is a basis of truth in what it is trying to communicate to us. No one likes to be bullied or shamed, and our "should" or "need to" voice is an excellent bully and well versed in the art of shaming.

Another frequently used thought pattern or inner voice is our "justification" voice. It typically immediately follows our "should" voice. It doesn't like the bullying of the "should" thought pattern and tries to defend you. The justification voice can be just as detrimental to your well-being and can head you down the path of procrastination, blaming or victimhood.

"You don't have to do the take out the trash tonight. So what if the pickup is tomorrow, you can do it in the morning. After all, you work hard and deserve a rest."

"You have done nothing that needs an apology. In fact, she owes an apology to you! If she can't handle the truth, that's her problem." (Often used after you criticize or shame someone else by telling them what they *should* or *need to* do as a way to manage your own fear or judgment of them.)

"You can call your mom later; you don't need to listen to her complain after the day you've had."

"You deserve a treat. Go ahead and enjoy yourself! You can start the diet tomorrow."

Resisting the "should" voice and not wanting to think about negative consequences of our actions is one reason people procrastinate. They don't want to be controlled by a bully who uses negative drama to control them with fear. They give in to the justification voice, which pretends there is no problem or better yet, the problem is the other person. The push/pull paradox between the two can be paralyzing.

But far more detrimental to our overall emotional health than the "should" or "justification" voices, is the critical thought path or the inner critical voice. Our inner critic is the part of the emotional center where we take our negative experiences from birth to present day, assign blame and make decisions about how to protect ourselves or control our environment, so we never have to be hurt again.

The inner critical voice is the evil nemesis of self-compassion. Worry, anxiety, stress, and self-doubt are the companions of the critical inner voice. Together they foster self-criticism, distrust, withdrawal, self-limitation, perfectionism and addictions.

The inner critical voice targets relationships and how others view you. It tells you not to get too close, or you're going to get hurt. The fear of abandonment or being alone is genuine.

Negative thought patterns can result in an inner monologue that criticizes in a scathingly cruel, berating manner. But in addition to criticizing, it partners with the self-protection of justification, everyone's inner best friend, to create an emotional wall of self-protection.

Your inner critical thought pattern will tell you that "no one will ever care about you" or "if he knew what you were really like, he would leave you" and then adds "You're better off alone, you don't need a relationship, you can take care of yourself."

Emotionally unavailable people emotionally abuse themselves. And since the negative thought processes are basing your thoughts on relational experiences that have some basis in fact, it's hard to shut down the inner critical voice. Unless you are willing to genuinely facing the fear and pain and let it go, the defense is to blame and self-protect.

Self-compassion breaks the self-fulfilling cycle of the inner critical thought pattern. The first step in self-compassion is learning to recognize when the inner critical voice is speaking.

"You are so stupid!"

"You will never be loved!"

"You'll never be in a relationship."

"You'll always be alone'"

"You've screwed up your children; where did you go wrong?"

"Why did you do that? You are so dumb."

"Have a drink, and you'll feel better."

"You'll never get promoted; you will be stuck here forever."

"If they knew what your house looked like they would be appalled."

"If he knew you were struggling financially, it would be over!"

"You'll never be accepted."

"They're more successful than me because they had better parents."

"You blew your one chance."

"All the good ones are in a relationship already. You'll be alone forever, and it's your entire fault."

"Who would want you?"

"If you had a better childhood or support, your life would be better."

I could fill an entire book with negative thought pattern examples. Identifying when your inner critical voice in charge is easy; learning to stop listening to that voice is hard and takes practice. Your negative thought patterns are trying to protect you from being hurt and in the process, it hurts you. Crazy, right?

Many women drivers will automatically throw their right arms out across the passenger seat whether it's occupied or not when they have to brake the car suddenly. It's a protective reaction that is almost impossible to control even though studies show that in the event of an actual accident the airbag will hit their arm and force it into the passenger that causes the injury they are attempting to prevent.

The bottom line is we have negative things which we believe about ourselves based on our past experiences, and the inner critical voice never wants us to experience that pain again. It either tries to preempt the pain by saying the negative thing to ourselves where it feels like we have more control or tries to convince us to withdraw from the potential pain, real or perceived.

After we learn to recognize the inner critical voice and stop allowing it to control us, the second step in self-compassion is to tell ourselves the truth. Many people feel like they were not loved, not cared for, not accepted, or stupid in childhood. They had to become self-reliant to survive. Acknowledging the truth about the way you feel about yourself and attempting to trace that back through your personal history can be scary but liberating.

Jason grew up in a lower-middle-class family. His mother stayed home and raised their five children while his dad worked at the mill. He grew up and became an attorney. He thought he had the idyllic life; comprised of two children, a dog and a house with a picket fence. He was stunned when his wife of sixteen years served him divorce papers. Sure his wife nagged him quite a bit, about his drinking, childish behavior, permissive parenting, porn and TV watching but he never saw it coming. He was so hurt by the divorce he was unable to ever have a successful relationship again.

His critical inner voice told him that he was never going to be able to live up to the expectations a new partner would put on him. If they found out who he really was, they would leave too. He spent years recovering financially from the divorce and rebuilding his retirement account.

He was lonely, and he enjoyed sex, but he told himself fiercely he was fine on his own. He never saw himself wanting a relationship again for the rest of his life, but he was lonely, enjoyed regular sex, and there was a part of him that wanted companionship. Occasionally he dated. However, the minute he thought it was getting serious he broke it off, usually not before his dating partner had fallen in love with him, leaving her devastated.

Jason wasn't telling himself the truth. As an adult, he enjoyed a good relationship with his parents and siblings, but his childhood was not nearly as idyllic as he says it was. His father spent a lot of time working, and when he was home, he withdrew. His mother was left to cope with raising five children on a meager budget. She was the cook, cleaner, disciplinarian, bill payer, budget master and the sole decision-maker. This left her filled with anxiety, and when she felt stressed, she got angry and yelled. She yelled a lot.

Jason would never admit this to his family, but he felt on his own as a child unable to please an overbearing, stressed-out mother and an absent father. He learned that he would have to take care of himself to survive.

The feelings he had from childhood transferred into his marriage and onto his wife. He withdrew, drank too much and was a permissive parent. His wife felt alone in the union. She felt less like his wife than his mother. After spending years lonely in the marriage relationship and trying to address this to no avail, she gave up.

The pain of the divorce was so hurtful emotionally and financially to Jason that he vowed never to be hurt again. Even though he honestly did want a successful relationship, he committed to being alone for the rest of his life. If he had used self-compassion to address how he felt inadequate and unaccepted as a child, he would not have had employed so many defense mechanisms to distance himself from his wife, and they probably would be together today.

Self-compassion is gently owning up to your mistakes and conversely, not taking the blame for other's mistakes. Telling yourself the truth about your feelings, even if it is painful, is a critical key in loosening their grip over your reactions.

The third step in self-compassion is acknowledging the pain rather than medicating it. Everyone has wounds that can then lead to limiting self-beliefs. Anyone who has ever had a deep cut knows that cleaning the wound stings. Thinking back to traumatic events, hurtful incidences, times you felt stupid, or alone can be very uncomfortable.

Acknowledge:

You were hurt, and it was wrong.

You are worth being treated better than you are being treated.

You have value.

The incident caused you to believe false things about yourself that you need to let go of.

The fourth step in self-compassion is to forgive yourself. Victims of incest can blame themselves as a way to control the pain because somehow it seems safer than blaming the predator who hurt them. At the root of everything, what your inner critical voice throws at you is shame. The person you blame most is you for not protecting yourself well enough, as if you could.

That's a mistake the emotionally unavailable person is sure not to make again, triggering the over-deployment of defense mechanisms or medicating by substance abuse or checking out. The underlying reaction is "You can't hurt me if I withdraw." If you forgive yourself and others, you will not need to retreat out of fear you're going to get hurt.

The final step in practicing self-compassion is letting go of self-limiting beliefs.

"You will never find love."

"You'll never get married again."

"You'll never succeed at_____."

"You are so stupid."

"It will never work out for you."

Stop the self-pity and beating up on yourself NOW. It's just as easy to believe the positive as the negative; it just *doesn't feel as safe*. Opening yourself up to new possibilities can be exciting and fun. Life is not through with you! When negative self-talk rears its ugly voice in your head, shut it down. Refuse to participate in the conversation.

Practicing self-compassion is:

1. Recognizing the inner critical thought paths.

2. Accepting what core beliefs are correct and rejecting the lies.

3. Acknowledge the pain and letting the wounds heal.

4. Forgiving yourself and others.

5. Letting go of self-limiting beliefs.

Ways to practice and work with yourself on self-compassion:

1. Stop the should-*ing*

Consider the vast chasm between the words "should" and "could."

Should:

...is a bully.

...treats you like a child.

...uses guilt or fear as a motivator.

...makes you feel stupid and leaves you with a sense of failure.

... Demands its own way.

... Elicits anger, stubbornness, or rebellion.

Could:

... Asks a question.

...Gives you options.

... Treats you like an adult.

... Allows you to make your own decision.

... Elicits thought, not reaction.

Work on eliminating the word "should" (or need to) from both your internal and external vocabularies meaning stop abusing yourself and others with your bullying judgment. Every time you find yourself using the word "should" immediately replace it with the word "could." Every time you find yourself say "you need to" or "I need to" immediately replace it with "would you consider" in the sentence. Turn the edict into a respectful question. Not only will this exercise help you treat others with respect, drastically reducing conflict, but it can also dramatically change your inner monologue.

Consider the difference between the following sentences:

"You *should* call your mother."

"You *could* call your mother."

"You *should* lose weight."

"*Could* you commit to eating healthy today?"

"You need to stop eating so much."

"Would you consider smaller portions?"

"You need to stop letting him treat you that way!"

"Would you consider that you have value and are worth respecting?"

Could you stop forcing yourself to do things you dread by changing the way you speak to yourself? Could you allow yourself and others to have feelings and thoughts? Could you treat yourself and others with love by asking rather than ordering them to perform?

Making the could/should shift costs you nothing and can dramatically reduce the tension during your interactions with others. Not allowing the inner critical voice to control you or others with guilt and fear-inducing "should" sentences, is priceless. And if you can make the shift in your thinking, this one relational change alone could be worth the cost of this entire book.

2. Silencing the inner critic.

The next time you feel stupid, embarrassed, or find yourself excoriating yourself, ask your inner critic this, "tell me what you want me to do differently next time?" Once you've listened to your inner critic, tell it to shut up because you don't want to hear the criticism anymore.

The reason the inner critic has such control is that it's often genuinely right. Call your mom, maintain a healthy weight, not drinking too much, being loving to your partner are all good things. But our negative thought patterns shame and bully us and others rather than helping us to move forward in a positive, healthy way.

Forcing those negative thought patterns from browbeater into cheerleader can be a powerful force for self-love and change.

Inner voice: Good going, that was embarrassing.

Self: What do you want me to do differently next time?

Inner voice: Four suggestions for handling things differently.

Self: Great. I got it. I don't want to hear about this incident again.

Imagine your inner critic dressed as a cheerleader instead of your disapproving parent or coach or drill sergeant. Shift that inner critic from:"You failed, you worthless idiot" to "You'll get it next time, I believe you can improve."And then don't criticize yourself for the incident again. Break the power of shame because you dealt with it, you learned from it and it's over.

3. End the cycle

When you find yourself criticizing or shaming yourself, follow the five steps to end the cycle:

1. Recognize when the inner critical thought path is speaking.

2. Accept what is true and reject lies, get rid of judgments, or assumptions.

3. Acknowledge the pain and let the wounds heal.

4. Forgive yourself and others.

5. Do not engage in self-limiting beliefs.

Chapter Eight:
Reactions: Dealing with Your
Defense Mechanisms.

In the war against emotional unavailability, defense mechanisms play a primary role. We all use defense mechanisms in our daily life when conflict arises. The emotionally unavailable person takes it a step further and uses defense mechanisms as a wall of withdrawal. Learning to manage our defense mechanisms is a critical key to overcoming emotional unavailability.

Most of us have heard the mantra; "Look both ways before you cross the street." Why? Our parents didn't want us to get hit by a car. We wear sunscreen to block out the sun's rays and prevent us from getting skin cancer. We wear seatbelts every time we drive the car, so we don't get hurt in a statistically improbable car accident. Much of what we do in our daily life is about not getting hurt.

The self-protection mode is real, not just physically but emotionally as well. The emotionally unavailable person is in hyper overprotection mode. They take standard emotional defense mechanisms to the extreme. The partner of the emotionally unavailable person reacts in fear of getting hurt with their own set of defense mechanisms. And now we have a cycle, a push-pull, of defense and withdrawal.

There are some great things about defense mechanisms as a coping tool. They help us survive and protect us from emotional pain. And to some degree, they act as a filter by which we can control our emotions.

On the flip side, there are some very negative consequences of living a life dependent upon defense mechanisms to manage our relationships.

Typically the cycle is conflict, followed by defense mechanism, and ending with withdrawal. This cycle will repeat itself until resolution takes place, whether that takes days or years.

Often people get so tired of being in this cycle that they prematurely end the relationship, not realizing they're going to face the same sequence in their next relationship and will continue to do so until they learn how to manage their defense mechanisms rather than being managed by them.

We employ defense mechanisms when we feel fearful, stressed, or attacked. We use them to control the other person or situation. Most people use a defense mechanism during a conflict and then let them go when a resolution presents itself whether it is a temporary or permanent resolution. The emotionally unavailable person never entirely turns off his or her defense mechanisms, they are always employing them.

The following is a list of the most common defense mechanisms employed in relationships. This list is not all-inclusive, there are other defense mechanisms, but these are the ones that seem to come in play most often in the relationships of the emotionally unavailable.

1. Aggression:

   - Intimidation.

   - Yelling.

   - Entering into someone's personal space.

   - Throwing things.

   - Stomping.

   - Slamming.

   - Scarring.

   - Bullying.

   - Threatening.

   - Controlling.

   - Judging.

- Ordering.

- Physically or emotionally abusing others.

2. Avoidance:

  - Procrastination.

  - Changing the subject.

  - Refusing to respond.

  - Remaining silent.

  - Making excuses or double booking on purpose.

  - Forgetting.

  - Declining to discuss an issue.

  - Lying instead of telling the truth to avoid conflict.

  - Refusing to take responsibility.

  - Pretending you're dumb.

  - Not telling the truth about how you feel.

  - Being complicit.

  - Refusing to take action or change.

3. Blaming:

- Refusing to accept responsibility for your actions.

- Distracting the conversation from your responsibility by shifting the focus to another person.

- Fake apologies.

4. Compartmentalization:

- Separating your choices or behaviors from your moral core or true self.

- Hiding your actions or choices from yourself or others.

5. Compliance:

- Going along to get along.

- Doing something that someone else wants even though you do not want to.

- Agreeing to end the conversation, even though you do not agree.

- Coupled with or resulting in passive-aggressive behavior.

- Choosing to be nice rather than deciding what is right for you.

6. Defiance:

- Refusing to acknowledge the truth or to take action to feel a sense of control even if it is detrimental to you or others.

7. Denial:

- Refusing to believe the truth.

8. Dependence:

- Asking someone else to fix or solve problems or situations that are your responsibility.

- Forfeiting adulthood because it's easier to have someone else make decisions or take responsibility.

9. Displacement:

- Expressing anger toward someone or something when you are upset about someone or something else.

10. Dissociation:

- The separation of being present and withdrawing into the mind.

- Being unable to remember a specific event or stressful experience.

- A person who can live in an emotional fantasy in their mind while still remaining physically present in reality.

- Being checked-out.

11. Escape:

- Refocusing your attention or avoiding a problem.

- Spending hours watching TV or playing video games.

- Abuse of drugs or alcohol.

- Moving from job to job without taking responsibility for your actions.

- Filling your time with excessive volunteering or work.

12. Hyper-vigilance:

- Perceiving a threat where none may exist.

- Over-controlling against an unseen or assumed danger.

- Insisting that everything is done *right* in order to ward off danger somehow.

13. Intellectualize:

- Staying in your head.

- Shutting down emotions.

- Approaching emotional situations with a clinical calmness that denies the gravity of the situation.

14. Internalizing:

- Stuffing down your feelings or thoughts and accepting another person's beliefs, thoughts, and actions as if they are your responsibility.

15. Isolation:

- Cutting off contact with people to feel safe or punish them.

- Becoming agoraphobic or quitting groups or not attending events to feel safe.

16. Lying:

- Avoiding taking responsibility for your actions by choosing not to tell the truth whether by commission or omission to avoid repercussions, real or perceived.

17. Managing:

- Taking another person's responsibility on by fixing something that they could do for themselves.

- Treating adults like children by over-explaining, over-planning, or by an overemphasis on negative consequences to force them to take action, even if that action is right for them. Refusing to let children mature into adults.

- Over-helping, or over-doing for someone able to do for themselves.

- Treating adults with disrespect by invalidating their concerns as them being dramatic, their viewpoint not important, or unnecessarily worried. Being dismissive of an adult's valid fears, concerns or feelings as a way of managing the situation and not addressing the actual problem.

- Becoming a martyr, or ignoring your own needs by being preoccupied with other's needs when they could be taking care of themselves.

- Controlling, manipulating or overly fixing.

- Making you the solution to a problem you did not create.

18. Minimizing:

- Downplaying your actions or the actions of others.

- Making something less than it really is.

- Justifying your actions or someone else's actions as less damaging than they are.

- Using criticism or judging an adult to prevent them from sharing a concern instead of dealing with the actual problem.

19. Perfectionism:

- Trying to be perfect to escape being judged.

- Judging others as less superior to you so that you feel better about yourself.

- Noticing every flaw and allowing the perceived flaws to diminish the value or a person or thing.

- Make judgments of worth about yourself or someone else based upon appearance, money, career, parenting style or material possessions.

20. Rationalizations:

- Telling yourself or someone else a story to justify your actions.

- Making up a reason for your actions that help you avoid responsibility for your own choices.

- Rationalizing your behavior.

21. Reaction Formation:

- Acting the opposite of the way you feel to appease a person or deny feelings to feel safe with the person with whom you have conflict.

- Acting overly fake or agreeable to a person with whom you are angry or hurt to not be wounded further or expressing any negative emotions that lead to further conflict with them.

22. Regression:

- Mature problem-solving methods are given up in favor of child-like ways of fixing problems.

23. Self-Hatred:

- Using self-flagellation or self-pity to avoid taking responsibility or face the truth.

- Playing the "I'm so stupid!" card to the point where the issue is unable to be addressed.

- A way of acknowledging behavior but not really changing it.

24. Withdrawal:

- Removing you or cutting someone off either physically or emotionally.

- Refusing to communicate as a means of punishment or self-protection.

Defense mechanisms are also called coping mechanisms or coping tools. When used correctly and for a limited time some defense mechanisms can keep us safe, either emotionally or physically.

Using intellectualization during a medical emergency can be extremely helpful. Continuing to do so after the crisis is over is not. Distancing yourself is a great short-term strategy, but it will emotionally cripple your ability to have an authentic relationship with prolonged use.

Emotional unavailability results when you use defense mechanisms as a life-long strategy to avoid emotional pain.

The average person doesn't carry around a list of defense mechanisms to select one to use in a particular interaction. Defense mechanisms are reaction or overreaction to a threat real or perceived.

They are the emotional lava that flows out of a fear or pain volcano. Most people think that the defense mechanism or a reaction is the problem when in actuality it's the cover-up of the actual problem.

Most people get upset when someone uses the aggression defense mechanism of yelling or screaming at them. But when people yell or scream it is almost always about their internal fear.

They are afraid of being overwhelmed, exposed, found out, forced to create a solution they think is beyond them, feeling stupid and abandoned or confirmation that whatever they believe about themselves is true. The person who feels threatened tries to intimidate or back down the person they perceive is a threat. It is almost always about them, and almost never about you.

Most people would say the yelling is the problem, but yelling is the byproduct or result of the problem. The actual problem is whatever unwanted or scary emotion triggered a reaction.

People yell and scream to get heard. They are afraid that they're not going to be able to defend themselves or communicate in a way that gives validity to their viewpoint. People who get angry a lot and act out aggressively are afraid they have no value and are fighting an internal battle for that not to be true. Aggressive behavior is always about the internal pressure in the aggressor.

It's true that people can act with evil intention. Physical, sexual or emotional abuse is never okay for any reason. If you are being abused or are an abuser, please put down this book and get help right away.

People can act like jerks. They can be hurtful and just plain wrong. They can treat others, even people they love badly. Human beings are not perfect and they chose to do wrong things or act in an unloving manner.

Defense mechanisms are not an excuse or justification to hurt others or to be hurt.

In the context of helping someone overcome emotional unavailability, defense mechanisms both the positive and the negative aspects must be addressed. Because the reality is they are the wall that blocks an emotionally available relationship.

Emotional unavailability is using defense mechanisms to keep your partner or family at an emotional distance to manage your fear of getting hurt or abandoned and in the process creating the same pain you are seeking to avoid.

If you want to get past emotional unavailability and have an honest and caring relationship with someone you can trust, you and your partner both must deal with your defense mechanisms and address the role they play in your relationship.

Ways to work with your defense mechanisms:

1. Learning from conflict.

The next time you have a conflict take time to analyze what happened. What defense mechanism did you use? What defense mechanism did that the other person use? Ask yourself what the underlying fear or pain of each party was. Go back to the person you had a conflict with and take responsibility for your part in the conflict.

"I want to talk about the conflict we just had. I'm sorry I yelled (or left, stormed off, gave you the silent treatment or _____.) I've been working with myself on whether I have value (or self-worth, feeling dumb, feeling ugly, feeling unlovable or _____.) this situation tapped into that fear, and I reacted. I'm working on not doing that and learning to manage my fear a little better. I take responsibility for my reaction to the situation, and I apologize.

That's it. If you begin to take on your emotions, work with your reactions and to acknowledge what is true, you will be able to start to open up emotionally. You'll quiet the inner critic and be able to heal emotional pain.

Ideally, all the people involved in the conflict would be able to acknowledge their part in it. But it's not important that the other person responds with their own responsibility even if they were solely responsible for starting the conflict. It's not essential they reciprocate; it's crucial for you to recognize your thoughts and emotions are controlling you and take responsibility for that.

Sometimes the other person does not want to address their own inner turmoil and minimize the conflict or they try to stop the apology, or will become uncomfortable. The goal isn't to quell the conflict; it's to release your fear and negative self-beliefs. Carry on through their discomfort and take responsibility for how you felt and the reactions you had as a result of the way you think about yourself. It gets easier, I promise.

Occasionally I will recognize a reactive irritated, aggressive tone in my voice when I perceive someone is trying to manage me. Being treated like a child taps into my fear that the other person doesn't respect me and is trying to control me. I ought to be able to recognize that the other person trying to manage me is entirely about them managing their fear and not about me at all but instead I react.

I will stop the conversation right then and say, "Hey, sorry for the tone of voice in my last comment. I just had a bad moment to the way I perceived the conversation was going, and I'm sorry." Often the other person will express that they were not bothered by my tone.

Notice, I don't have to agree with what they were saying or do what they want. I'm merely acknowledging that I have reactions to being mistreated.

It's not essential that they were not bothered by my reaction nor that they didn't take responsibility for trying to manage me. What is important is that I recognized that my fear and my inner critical voice were trying to control me. I took responsibility and addressed the fear.

Another simple phrase I use to respond when I feel I am reacting to anxiety brought on by conflict with another person is: "That's good information."

The information I received is that the other party is reacting in fear and trying to place blame, responsibility or control me. This recognition that it's not my responsibility to fix a situation created by another person will ultimately lead to healthy self-worth. It also has the by-product of helping the other person to learn to stop managing other people and treat them like adults.

Wounded self-esteem heals slowly. It's in working with ourselves daily, discovering why we react and linking to our own inner emotional pressure points and then letting that pain go that a healthy sense self worth develops.

Accept the truth, discard the lies, and forgive yourself and others. Stop living like you either have something to prove or don't care what other people think, because both are lies you are telling yourself.

2. Identify your defense mechanisms:

While it's true that you can use any defense mechanism, most of us are prone to using a few specific ones regularly. Look through the list of defense mechanisms and identify the ones you use most often.

Things to work through:

- Why do you think you rely on those coping tools most often?

- Can you detect a pattern behind your use of defense mechanisms?

- Which coping tools does your partner use?

- Which coping tools did your parents and siblings use?

- What pain or fears could they have been avoiding?

- How did your parents or siblings use of defense mechanisms affect you?

- What did you learn from watching your parents use defense mechanisms?

- Are you taking on responsibility or allowing others' reactions to form self-beliefs about your worth?

- Can you acknowledge that stress, pain, and pressure cause you to interpret a situation to confirm your negative self-beliefs and react accordingly?

- Can you let go of responsibility for other people's reactions or defense mechanisms and take responsibility for yours?

Chapter Nine:
You're in Charge: Stopping your thoughts from controlling you.

In chapter nine we learned that our reactions and defense mechanisms are primarily based on what we think and feel rather than on the other person's words or actions.

Emotionally unavailable people are held captive in a prison of their thoughts. The way they think about themselves and the way they have chosen to interpret their life to this point has led them to conclude that the world is not a safe place. They believe that they are entirely worthy of rejection. As a result, their thought patterns force them into absolute emotional self-reliance.

The emotionally available person will make declarations, wearing them like a badge of honor: "I don't need anyone!" "I don't need a relationship." "I never want a relationship." "I can go through another divorce again; I just can't!" "I'm better off alone."

Fear of being abandoned emotionally, physically or financially is just too much for the emotionally unavailable person.

They self-reject before you have an opportunity to reject them, sadly bringing them not only loneliness but the very pain they seek to avoid. What's behind their self-rejection? Their negative thoughts or anxieties make them feel relationally hopeless. While there are true narcissists in the world, for many emotionally unavailable people, arrogance is a cover for insecurity. Emotionally unavailable people have a very negative inner thought life about themselves and often the world in general.

Psychiatrist Aaron T. Beck and his student David D. Burns pioneered the work of cognitive distortions. They identified destructive thought patterns that warp the way we interpret people and situations.

Since emotionally unavailable people feel they are unlovable, it stands to reason that they have negative thought patterns that foundationally impact their view of relationships. Challenging these beliefs is necessary to heal their ability to trust.

Thoughts lead to emotions.

Emotions lead to reactions.

Reactions lead to confirmation of the thought pattern.

Unless you challenge those thoughts, the cycle will begin again.

Negative thought patterns:

All-or-Nothing Thinking

Relegating all people and situations to a good/bad category:

- All women are gold diggers (Some women earn more than men. Maybe they like you for who you are.)

- All divorce is bad. (All divorce is emotionally painful but not necessarily bad or failure and in some cases, necessary.)

- All men cheat. (Many men and women are faithful, loving partners.)

- I always fail. (I make my share of mistakes, but I learn from them and move on.)

Overgeneralizing:

The belief that once something happens, it will always happen.

- Since my first wife left me, any subsequent marriage will end in divorce. (A lie people tell themselves all the time.)

- All men will cheat on me. (Not all men or women cheat.)

- Having a relationship means giving up all my freedom. (You can have a relationship and not feel suffocated.)

Discounting the Positive:

If a good thing happens, deciding it doesn't count or must not be significant:

- Just because I had a great date doesn't mean she likes me, it was a fluke. (Maybe she does like you, why don't you ask?)

- Just because my children had a lovely dinner with my girlfriend doesn't mean they want me to date. (Children want their parents to be happy. Why not ask how they feel about it?)

- Just because she seems nice doesn't mean she is she won't make demands of me soon. (Not all men or women are demanding or hide their true selves.)

Jumping to Conclusions

Responding to a situation before you have all the information:

- The person I am interested in never returned my call because he thinks I'm unattractive and dumb. (Or they didn't get the message, lost the number or had an emergency.)

- That person cut me off in traffic because they are a jerk! (Or they are late for work and are going to be fired; they didn't see you in their car mirror's blind spot; are lost and making mistakes in navigation; they are a teen or geriatric driver; they are having a bad day and didn't see you.)

Mind Reading

Without any evidence, deciding that you know how someone else is feeling or what they are thinking:

- She must be mad at me to look at me that way. (Or she's lost in thought; replaying a confrontation with someone else in her mind; trying not to sneeze; thinking about her sick cat.)

- He blames me. (Or he blames himself and is too embarrassed to talk about it.)

- That person thinks I'm a loser; I'll never be as good as him. (He probably thinks you feel the same way about him.)

Fortunetelling

The belief that you know the future based on past experiences.

- I'm never going to find someone who loves me. (You have to be open to being loved but it is possible. There is someone for everyone.)

- If I marry, it will end in divorce. (Or you could meet someone who is an excellent fit for you and be happy for the rest of your life.)

Magnifying (Catastrophizing) or Minimizing

The act of putting too much emphasis on the importance of positive or negative thoughts or events believing they create a direct cause and effect.

- I said the wrong thing to him, and now he will not want to be with me. (One utterance does not make or break a relationship.)

- If she knew about my debt, she would stop dating me. (Lots of people are in debt and are in relationships.)

- I'm bald. No one will ever find me attractive. (Bruce Willis, Vin Diesel, Dwayne Johnson, Patrick Stewart. My brother. People date people who are bald. Some people find it sexy.)

- I can't date her because if we get married and divorced, then I will lose my retirement. (How about you start with a first date? Ever heard of a prenup? How do you know that you will end up marrying or divorcing?)

- She's more successful because she had a better childhood than I did. (Everyone is responsible for their own success.)

- Stop worrying or it will happen. (Lots of things we worry about never happen. Sometimes worrying is a natural reaction to a stressful situation. It's being human.)

- It's ridiculous that you're concerned about _____. (Fear is a real thing and denying it does not alleviate it. Making people feel foolish about their concerns invalidates their feelings and is unloving.)

Emotional Reasoning

Believing that if something feels true it is true.

- I feel like a failure, and I am a failure. (I've suffered a setback; it's going to get better.)

- I feel ugly because I am ugly. (I am okay the way I am.)

- I feel unlovable because I am unlovable. (I am worth loving.)

- I feel so stupid because I feel like I shouldn't make silly mistakes. (Everyone makes errors; take responsibility, learn and move on.)

- I worried about that and it happened. (You don't have that kind of power.)

Labeling (or Mis-Labeling)

Negatively labeling a person rather than characterizing their behavior or a mistake.

- She's a bad person (It was wrong of her to lie.)

- I'm stupid (I left my shopping list at home, it will be okay.)

- I'm a loser (You went through a divorce, lots of people have. It does not define you.)

Personalization

Assigning blame to yourself even though you were not responsible, making it about you.

- It's my fault he hits me. (It is not your fault, get out and get help now.)

- My father or mother is unhappy because of me. (They are responsible for their own happiness.)

- I have to fix this situation. (Everyone is responsible for themselves.)

- They're threatened by me. (They are reacting out of their own pain or fear which in reality has nothing to do with you.)

Emotionally unavailable people have a high level of anxiety which manifests itself in negative thought patterns. Recognizing that you have these negative thought processes and that you may be acting or reacting on cognitive distortions is a huge step forward toward becoming emotionally available.

These distortions can primarily impact reactions and the ability to trust because we perceive that they are confirmation of the lies we tell ourselves. Emotionally unavailable people must begin to challenge their cognitive distortions. Take responsibility for what is true, reject what is not.

Rejecting negative thought patterns or cognitive distortions can help a person break down the wall of self-protection that they perceive is necessary not to get hurt further. It's as if the emotionally unavailable person locks themselves in a room to escape an ax-murderer only to discover that they, themselves are the ax-murderer. Ouch.

Recognizing that your thoughts can be your most significant source of emotional pain can be overwhelming and a little hard to believe.

Consider someone experiencing PTSD. The traumatic event is over, but the feelings and coping mechanisms are present and doing the current emotional damage all in the name of self-protection.

The emotionally unavailable person is being held captive by reliance on cognitive distortions for emotional self protection.

Good news! You control those beliefs yourself, so you are the one that has the power to break them!

Take your erroneous beliefs head-on. Work through them until they no longer have control of your thoughts because those thoughts are your current emotional reality.

Ways to work on Cognitive Distortions:

1. Keep a log.

When you have a negative thought don't challenge it, just jot it down. Keep track of these thoughts for a week.

Note:

What patterns do you see?

Are you telling yourself the truth?

Do you see your life as happy and improving or lonely and sad?

2. Talk back to yourself.

When a negative thought arises, immediately reject it. Offer a different or more reasonable explanation to the thought. Do not allow false assumptions to rule you. Commit to telling yourself the truth. Do NOT let yourself interpret life through cognitive distortions.

3. Eliminate negative or toxic people from your life.

Misery loves company. If you have non-important people in your life that are ruled by cognitive distortions eliminate or minimize their role in your life. Avoid people with whom you feel you have to earn their approval.

4. Keep a success journal.

Jot down all of your success on any given day. Take note of every time you did something right or were kind.

5. Forgive yourself.

Forgive yourself for not being perfect. Allow yourself room to make mistakes. Make your life goal not to be perfect but always to be learning.

Chapter Ten:
How to Get More Help and Heal Quickly.

Is there a cure for emotional unavailability? Yes. Human beings can set aside self-protection, become trusting and experience fulfilling, loving relationships. It isn't an overnight cure but a process. If an emotionally unavailable person commits to working with him or herself, stopping their fears and anxieties from ruining their relationships, they can become emotionally available.

I know, because hundreds and hundreds of people have.

If they can do it, you can do it too!

You can have healthy relationships and be happy.

To start, take one chapter of the second part of this book and begin working on yourself in one area of your life.

If you are unable or unwilling to go to counseling and are ready to overcome emotional unavailability, I offer an affordable, step-by-step self-help course designed to guide you through a series of actions and put you on the *fast track* to emotional availability.

6 Workbooks with 48 lessons that will change your life.
www.ThePositiveRelationship.com

Becoming Your Emotionally Available Authentic Self is focused on moving you forward – fast! Easy to read and understand, the goal is to create significant change in your life in 30 days for $97.

All our courses are workbook style. They get right to the point and provide specific advice that is easy to do with worksheets, exercises.

Visit my website at www.ThePositiveRelationship.com to get more information

I do work privately with coaching clients. If you're interested in working with me, go to www.ThePositiveRelationship.com

Please remember that due to the volume, it takes some time, but I do answer every email I receive through my website. Visit www.ThePositiveRelationship.com and click on the "contact me" tab!

Thank you for purchasing The Cure for Emotional Unavailability. I know you could have picked any number of books to read, but you picked this book and for that I am extremely grateful.

I hope that it added at value and quality to your everyday life. If so, it would be so kind of you could share this book with your friends and family by posting to Facebook and Twitter.

If you enjoyed this book and found some benefit in reading this, I'd like to hear from you and hope that you could take some time to post a review on Amazon. Your feedback and support will help me get the message out there that healthy, satisfying relationships are possible. I value your insight to greatly improve my writing craft for future projects and make this book even better.

My heart is for you, and I wish you all the best in your future success!

Made in the USA
Coppell, TX
26 March 2024

30548937R00085